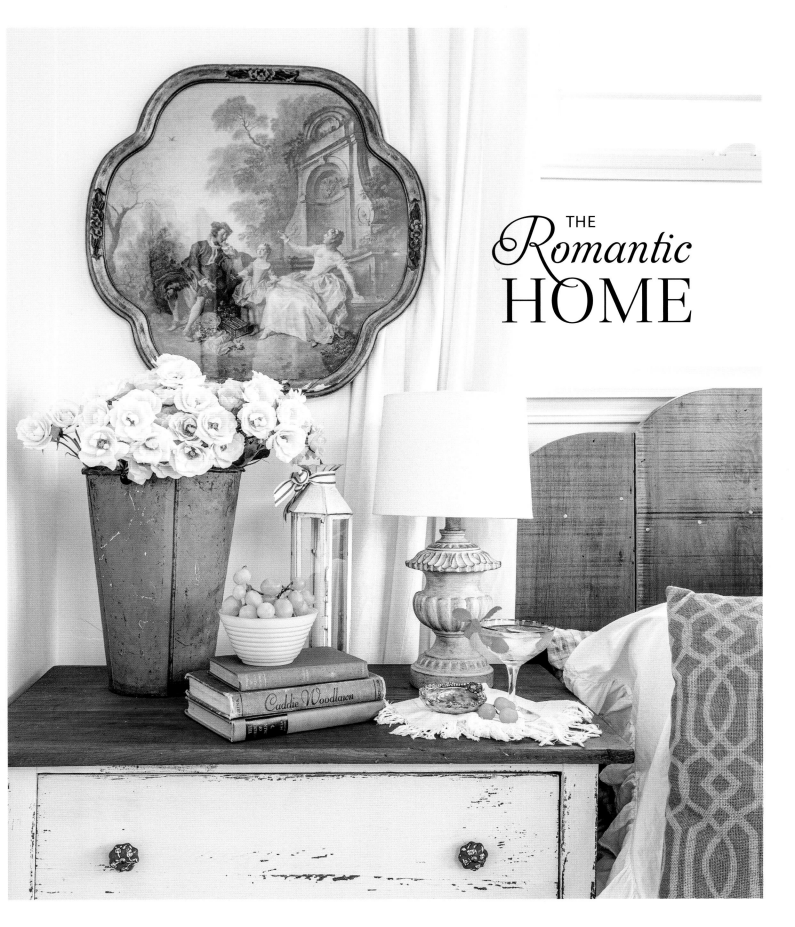

THE
Romantic
HOME

THE *Romantic* HOME

CELEBRATING PAST & PRESENT DESIGN

Fifi O'Neill

With photography by
MARK LOHMAN

RYLAND PETERS & SMALL
LONDON • NEW YORK

Senior designer Toni Kay
Editor Sophie Devlin
Production manager Gordana Simakovic
Senior commissioning editor Annabel Morgan
Art director Sally Powell
Creative director Leslie Harrington

Published in 2024 by Ryland Peters & Small
20–21 Jockey's Fields
London WC1R 4BW
and
341 East 116th Street
New York, NY 10029

www.rylandpeters.com

Text copyright © Fifi O'Neill 2024
Design copyright © CICO Books 2024
Photography by Mark Lohman copyright
© CICO Books 2024
Additional photography by John Ellis copyright
© John Ellis 2024
For photography credits, see page 160.

10 9 8 7 6 5 4 3 2 1

ISBN 978-1-80065-309-2

A CIP record for this book is available
from the British Library.

Library of Congress CIP data
has been applied for.

Printed and bound in China

MIX
Paper from
responsible sources
FSC® C106563

Contents

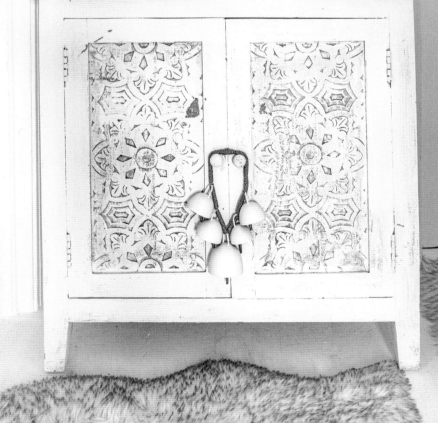

Introduction

Who doesn't long for a little more romance in their life? The type that makes your heart feel at ease when you walk into your home. It only takes a few elements to create a charmingly seductive and unexpected aesthetic, as original as it is restful, that makes any room beat to the gentle rhythm of home.

Romantic interiors come in many forms, but all share a common thread: the pursuit of beauty. With sentimental objects, fresh flowers, expressive art and whisper-soft colors, you can impart loveliness and personal flair to any room. It's a gentle, tender and thoughtful style that embodies the love of home and is always unique to the individual.

I believe in decorating your spaces with meaningful treasures that honor the past as well as the present, yet pedigree is never the main concern—love is. Graceful furnishings and exquisite finishing touches unite to create emotions, individuality and comfort, soothe the soul and foster contentment.

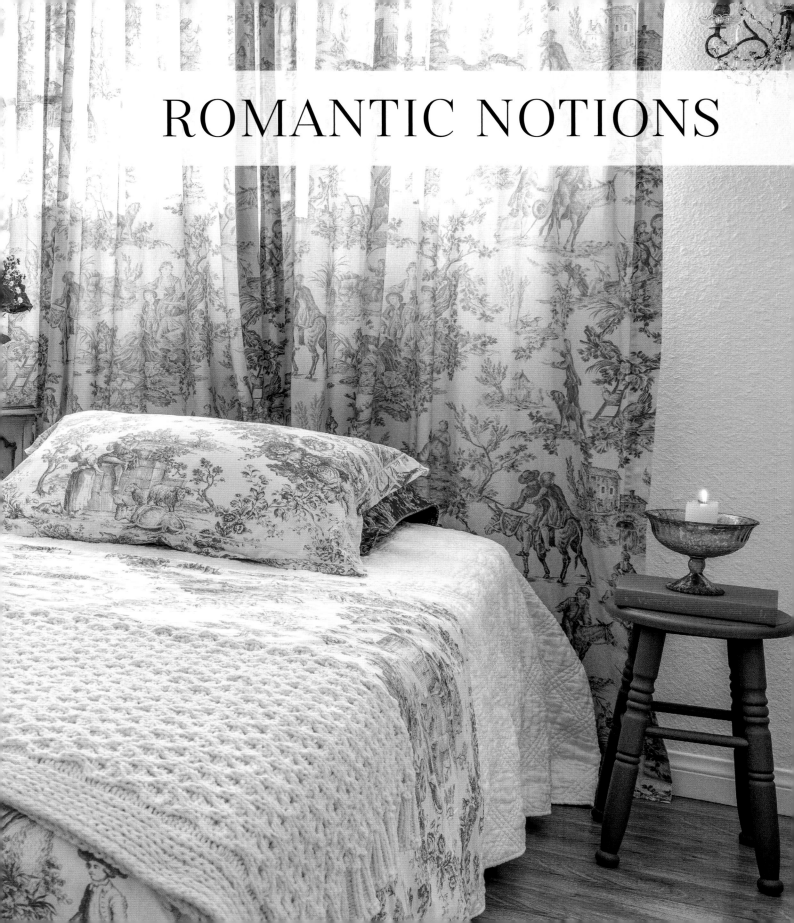

ROMANTIC NOTIONS

Colors

"Colors, like features, follow the changes of the emotions." **PABLO PICASSO**

espite their soft-spoken demeanor, subdued hues and pale pastels can pack a dramatic punch and make a discreet but consequential statement. Misty blues, blushing pinks, faded greens, barely-there lavenders and chalky grays rank high on the list of favorites. When paired with pristine, pearlescent whites, they epitomize romance and femininity. Their delicate presence conspires to create charming, relaxed and inviting spaces, may they be modest or grand.

It is well known that colors, tints, shades and tones have the power to influence emotions and transform any room from ordinary to magical. But softer hues have the unique ability to create a romantic atmosphere, especially when mixed with evocative items. Aqua elements look enchanting against a white palette in this bathroom (opposite). From furnishing to accessories, mellow shades of green such as seafoam, sage, olive and celadon bring a refreshing feeling while imparting a sense of renewal because of their intimate connection to nature (above).

Classic love stories always have partners who are perfectly suited to each other, and so it is with the enduring union of blue and white (left & below left). For a twist on the beloved combination, lilac and lavender are affable mates, or you can embrace a pure white palette (below). From shell pink to cherry blossoms, soft pinks have a rosy disposition. Mixed with vintage, pink goes beyond feminine and becomes truly timeless. A tonal palette and black accents keep pinks from seeming girlish and the look fresh and current (opposite).

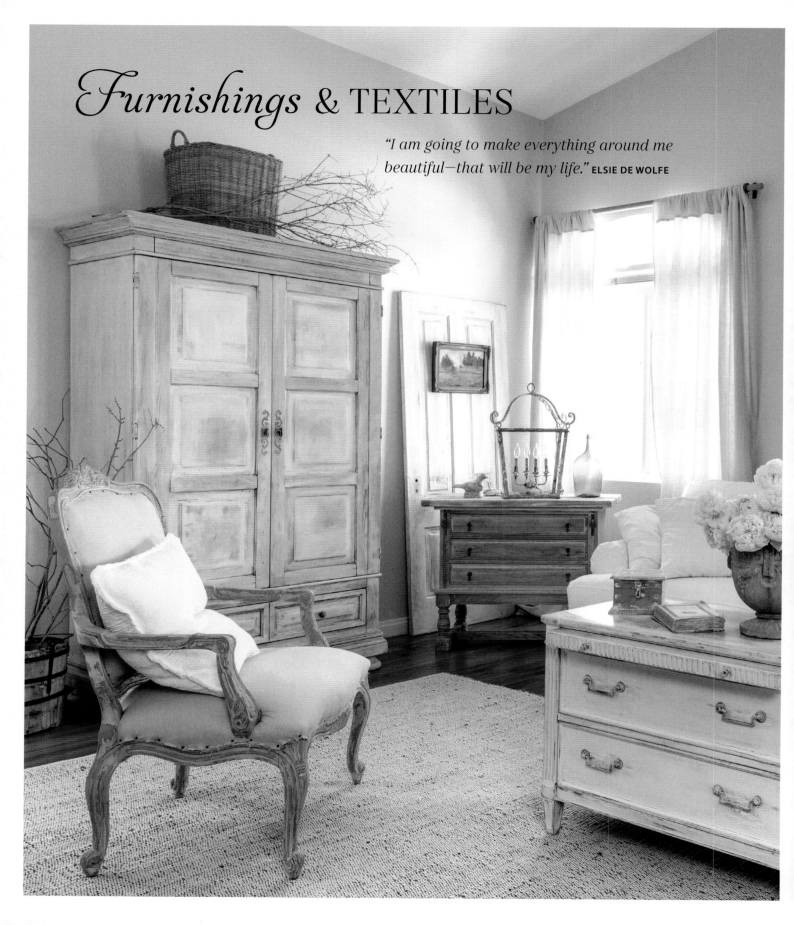

Furnishings & TEXTILES

"I am going to make everything around me beautiful—that will be my life." **ELSIE DE WOLFE**

*F*urnishings collected over time often bear a gentle patina and graceful lines that evoke the past with understated elegance. However, if they are curvy and soft, current pieces are a nice counterpoint to vintage ones, as they keep the decor from being staid and add just the right amount of whimsy. They also make good companions for vintage fabrics that evoke a feeling of age.

Like old friends with a story to tell, furnishings with a past have a natural appeal that kindles emotion and brings a hint of heritage to your home (opposite & above). The examples shown here easily marry rustic and refined sensibilities with an edge of sophistication. Their personality creates a chic atmosphere that is neither too curated nor too perfect. Fabrics with texture—think homespun linen, supple velvet, fine silk and tapestries—and patterns such as toile de Jouy, stripes, checks and florals have a subtle but unquestionable romanticism.

Demure, flamboyant or unruly, flowers and their fragrances make a lasting impression as well as adding charm and enhance a room's aesthetic appeal. Whether they spill softly from an ironstone pitcher or a crystal vessel, floral displays have the ability to exude a particular sentiment that no other decorative element can. Delicately scented or headily perfumed blooms that feel soft and old-fashioned have an undeniable romantic eloquence. Think of voluptuous peonies, fairylike hollyhocks, aromatic lilacs, lissome flowering branches and, of course, redolent roses.

Flowers have had their own language for thousands of years (left, below left & opposite). Though each has a specific meaning, some hold unmistakable terms of endearment. Just as their fragrance is fundamental to setting the mood of a room, so is the way they are presented. Whether a single bud in a vase, a grouping of similar blooms, a free-form arrangement lush with wild abandon or a bountiful bouquet, what matters is creating a thoughtful composition that appears natural and effortless.

Florals &
FRAGRANCES

"I must have flowers, always and always." **CLAUDE MONET**

Romantic visual clues are generally easy to detect, whereas fragrances can be much more elusive (below, right & below right). But whether they emanate from flowers or candles, exquisite scents are a magical manifestation of romance. They do more than adding beauty to rooms, contributing a subtle aroma that sets a mood and establishes a connection with nature. Floral fragrances are as quixotic and uplifting as a fresh-picked bouquet, and the final flourish that makes a home a sanctuary.

The most evocative floral displays are those with texture—it may come from silky rose petals, fragrant honeysuckle vines or upright stems of lavender, to name a few examples. But even one single aromatic peony, tuberose or hydrangea blossom with layers of ruffled petals will set the tone for an entire space.

Mirrors

*"Mirror, mirror on the wall,
who in this land is fairest of all?"*

THE BROTHERS GRIMM

*O*rnate and gilded or simply framed, vintage or new, mirrors
are indeed bewitching. They dazzle and delight and elevate
the aura of an interior. Their presence contributes much more than
reflection, light and dimension. They are statement pieces that
double as aesthetic accents. When showcasing a scene from a room,
they become works of art. If leaned against a wall, floor mirrors
expertly toe the line between appearing perfectly carefree and
expertly styled. Mirrors with a distressed or antiqued finish bounce
light in a gentle manner and add a slightly mysterious edge.

Statement mirrors are more than decorative accents. They
are central to the aesthetic of a room. When informally
propped on furniture, they create a sense of deconstructed
grandeur, an off-the-cuff elegance and a luxurious effect
(opposite). A large mirror can have a transformative impact
not only by providing additional dimension to a space but
also by bestowing architectural character where none exists
(above left). Ornate frames with intricate carvings and details
add a dramatic element that emulates a regal and fanciful
style, especially in a metallic finish against a contrasting
white background (above right).

Lighting

"Just as one candle lights another and can light thousands of other candles, so one heart illuminates another heart and can illuminate thousands of other hearts." **LEO TOLSTOY**

*N*othing imbues a room with a soft and utterly luxurious ambience like the glow from diffused light. Chandeliers and wall sconces with crystal pendants add sparkle, lamps with rosy shades invite intimacy, flickering candles suggest a sultry vibe and dainty strings of fairy lights play a key role in the making of a romantic space. Lights of all kinds are essential to set a mood that envelops rooms in a dreamy atmosphere.

Lighting has the capacity to create an atmosphere and mood, so it is vital to achieving an inviting and enchanting aura in your space in harmony with its function. When seeking that ethereal radiance, large or small glittering chandeliers have long been the crown jewels of the genre (opposite). However, these perennial favorites have a long list of equally effective and attractive romantic rivals, from branching wall sconces to vintage candelabras and twinkling tealights (above).

The sophisticated fixtures shown on these pages are the epitome of romanticism and glamour. From glimmering mercury glass candleholders (above left) to a wrought-iron lantern (left) and luxurious lamps dressed in elegant ostrich feathers or exotic animal print (above & opposite), they offer as many styles, materials and finishes as they do options. Alternatively, strings of lights can be draped over a bed to form a canopy or concealed behind a sheer fabric to create a dramatic headboard-like feature with a subtle sparkle. Whatever the accessory of choice, it's all about the glow.

*A*lluring and captivating decorative embellishments, may they be gleaming baubles, priceless keepsakes or relics bearing the inherent beauty conferred by time, hold more than stories. These fetching pieces imbue rooms with layers of sentiment that effortlessly bridge the gap between old and new, serious and fanciful.

Home is the place where you have total freedom to express your personality. And for those with tender souls, that often means a starring role for accessories that highlight their sentimental disposition. These finishing touches are the icing on the cake. Found objects, collectibles, artworks, mementos and a plethora of other items are curated into meaningful vignettes that tell a story (above & opposite). While some may be purely ornamental, others are meant to evoke a time and place.

Finishing
TOUCHES

"Refinement creates beauty everywhere." **WILLIAM HAZLITT**

Details are what makes a house a home (left, below & opposite) and there is a multitude of ways to add finishing touches, though quite often they are influenced by the function of the space. While living rooms make splendid settings for items that recall travels and events, bedrooms tend to be where plush throws and pillows are the accents of choice, where symbolic artworks add to the restful mood and infuse the space with a sense of soul. In the end, what's most important is to include objects not for their value but for what they mean to you.

THE HOMES

CHAPTER 1
Reclaimed Romance

Restored
TO BEAUTY

FOR MANY YEARS BEFORE SHE BOUGHT IT, TERESA DEJARLAIS WOULD GAZE LONGINGLY AT THIS THREE-STORY 1902 BRICK BUILDING IN BUFFALO, MINNESOTA. SHE DREAMED OF LIVING IN A PERIOD HOME WITH LINEAGE AND CHARACTER, AND THIS WAS EXACTLY WHAT SHE HAD IN MIND. AS FATE WOULD HAVE IT, TERESA EVENTUALLY REALIZED HER DREAM, THOUGH IT TOOK SEVERAL YEARS MORE BEFORE SHE WOULD TRULY BE ABLE TO CALL THIS PLACE HOME.

Located within walking distance of the city's historic center, just up the hill from Buffalo Lake, Teresa's home has an enviable view and an impressive footprint of 2,000 square feet/186 square meters on each of its three floors. "It's a grand old building with good bones and character, so I knew it would lend itself to a respectful, understated renovation," she says. "Throughout the years it had been home to several businesses, including a post office." But by the time Teresa took on this venerable building as a tenant, it was in dire need of an update. "I didn't yet own the building during the years of renovation," she says, "but I treated it as my own, always working toward that goal with the owners."

Teresa's business background and knowledge proved to be immensely helpful. It all began with her first trip to France in 1996 with her daughter Rachel and son Adam, which sparked her mad love affair with the country. Numerous trips later, Teresa is just as impassioned and there is no doubt that her travels have influenced her approach to design. She learned a lot about the business by buying at flea markets and selling in other people's shops.

ABOVE Teresa balances rustic and refined finishes throughout her home. This leaded-glass window makes a perfect foil for the chandelier and gently tarnished silverware—the floral centerpiece is one of Teresa's favorite finds. The dresser/chest of drawers and brick wall keep the vignette grounded.

OPPOSITE A French gilded mirror stars in the living room. Teresa's son Adam built the narrow console table from reclaimed wood. Positioned against the wall, it mimics a fireplace and allows Teresa to create displays based on the season or the mood of the moment. Vintage chairs add to the cozy setting.

"It's a grand old building with good bones and character."

THIS PAGE Exposed brick walls and 13-foot-/4-meter-high ceilings give the living room an expansive appeal. The antique daybed provides comfy seating and a sleeping spot for overnight guests. The neutral palette is punctuated with aqua, green and warm ocher accents from pillows and the painted fabric of the chair. Vintage doors and windows were made into cabinets to provide a staging area for oversized bottles and meaningful items.

LEFT Elegant hardware that Teresa brought back from Paris graces the door of one of the cabinets built by Adam. Delicate objects—statues, books, old house number plaques, wood carvings and more—found in flea markets and estate sales in France and locally are gathered on the shelves. They are safely stored yet easily accessible and clearly visible through the glass doors.

ABOVE Behind the dining-room table, Teresa has incorporated a rustic sideboard to provide space for buffet-style dinners and, when not in use, to display decorative items. The mirror's carved and gilded frame adds elegance to the setting.

OPPOSITE Teresa commissioned her nephew to make the dining table using the legs from another table. Adam then painted and waxed the surface of the wood. A mix of upholstered chairs and a rustic bench keeps the seating interesting. The architectural details on the walls are made of fiberglass and were found at an antiques store.

The two lower levels are now home to her own store, The Porch, which has become a much-loved Buffalo institution over the past 20 years. Teresa opened the doors to the retail space in 2003, the same year that she eventually bought the building from its previous owners. By this time, she says, "I had proven to myself that people liked the pieces I found and what my business had to offer, and that I could support myself doing it."

Her sense of style and her ability to let things unfold naturally is not just the secret to the success of The Porch, but also the essence of her top-floor home above the shop. The spacious loft was previously a mangled mess of plywood-paneled walls, drop ceilings and dated shag carpeting that masked the beauty she knew was there. With the help of Rachel, Adam and other skilled family members, Teresa started to reclaim and reveal the many hidden features. And so, the transformation began.

Removing plaster from the living room and bedroom walls uncovered the beautiful old bricks. The lower set of rafters were cut at a curved angle, creating an effect similar to the nave of a church, while old lath and plaster walls were left exposed and the ceilings were raised to a height of 12 feet/3.7 meters. An opening was cut into the dividing wall between the entrance and the living room to accommodate an arched, leaded-glass window, which brings ample sunlight into the foyer.

"It took 30 gallons of white paint—around 114 liters—just to clean up the place," Teresa recalls. "We also painted most of the floors a light gray and removed the linoleum in the kitchen.

OPPOSITE The kitchen renovation was a family affair. The stainless steel-topped island was discovered at a sale in Pine City, Minnesota. Teresa's nephew constructed the cabinets, using salvaged doors and windows, and installed the reclaimed sink. For a touch of industrial chic, Adam fashioned the light fixture and used recycled rafters from the living room to craft the countertop.

BELOW A fireplace fender that Teresa had for years has been upcycled as a pot rack in her well-organized kitchen. The plaster walls were left intact to contrast with the brick walls she uncovered in the living room and bedroom during the renovation. A shutter is propped against the wall as a unique display area.

This allowed us to restore the original wood flooring. Adam crafted the kitchen and living room cabinets out of vintage and salvaged materials."

Once the renovation was complete, she began to furnish her new home in a natural creamy palette. As a veteran shopkeeper, she has a talented carpenter and an upholsterer on hand who can make or remake anything she imagines. Secondhand chairs were reupholstered using old linen grain sacks and French vintage fabrics became pillows. Teresa bought pieces from estate sales, from the vendors whose wares are displayed in her store and from Adam, who sells vintage curiosities from a shop of his own called Twelve Vultures in nearby Minneapolis. She has layered in treasures from flea markets, including large bottles and jars, and silver items that add patina and history.

Today, Teresa is perfectly content living in the home, which she shares with her sister Jeanne. "In addition to being a great companion, Jeanne does a lot behind the scenes as well as helping in the shop." While the space is serenely styled, it is all done with functional daily living in mind and with the intention of making their family and friends feel welcome, never to impress. "I am truly living in my home and just being myself," Teresa says. "Everything here is secondhand or recast. Everything has been done as simply as possible with respect for the original. I try to use and be happy with what I have." Mission accomplished!

PAGE 42 To make the bath renovation affordable, Teresa painted the existing wall tiles white to match the tub and then added inexpensive white ceramic floor tiles. Above the wainscot, tiny mirror tiles add a sparkling touch. A tall, narrow iron stand is a space-saver and performs well for hanging bathrobes and towels.

PAGE 43 Layered over all-white linens, golden-hued French organza and a floral pillow add little touches of glamour to the bed. The nightstand was a long-ago find at a local antiques fair. Teresa kept its original finish, which echoes the weathered wood on the reupholstered chair. The curtains are hung with swing arms for maximum play of light.

OPPOSITE The sofa fits just right in the small living room and offers a cozy spot without taking up a lot of space. A varied mix of small items, interspersed with artwork from Deborah's collection, creates a gallery-like display. A stack of wicker chests plays double duty as side table and storage.

RIGHT Deborah kept the old English pine rustic table in the condition it was in when she bought it. Though different in style and finish, two vintage chairs complement a new pair from RH. The jute rug adds another layer of texture. The curvy chandelier contributes a discreet but elegant touch.

A Sentimental JOURNEY

FRAMED BY WILDFLOWERS AND A WHITE LATTICE FENCE, A LITTLE PINK STUCCO COTTAGE STANDS LIKE A VISION STRAIGHT OUT OF A FAIRY TALE. BUT WHEN DEBORAH AND HER HUSBAND DAVID FIRST LAID EYES ON THE QUAINT 73-YEAR-OLD SOUTHERN CALIFORNIA HOME, IT WASN'T QUITE AS CHARMING AS IT IS NOW, AND NEITHER WERE THE BARREN GROUNDS. STILL, THEY FELL IN LOVE WITH THE PROPERTY AND WITH THE BEAUTIFUL BEACHES AND HIKING TRAILS NEARBY.

The couple had little money to renovate, and most of the budget was spent on a new roof, fencing, plumbing and drainage. Nonetheless, they dreamed about transforming their newly acquired "diamond in the rough" into a romantic English cottage. With a little ingenuity, they were able to find some creative solutions. "The oak floors in the kitchen and eating area had been destroyed, and we couldn't afford to replace them with similar wood, so David put in basic, inexpensive tiles, which are still here today," Deborah explains.

Wherever possible, they adapted their vision to work with what they already had. "Those kitchen countertops are original to the house—they are over 70 years old and still in beautiful condition," says Deborah. "We don't mind having a few things that some would call dated. We chose comfort over the disruption and expense of a full remodel."

Deborah's heartfelt and somewhat nostalgic style makes one feel at home instantly. Upon entering the living room there is a sense of European flair and coziness stemming from the mix of character-rich English and French pieces and a gallery wall of antique artwork. "I love keeping nature-inspired art in the living room," explains Deborah, who used to have a small business selling vintage art and furniture over 20 years ago and has retained a number of works from the shop for her personal collection.

A few large pieces anchor this small room, including a large armoire that Deborah has painted in a muted shade of blue, a vintage Oushak rug and a tall, weathered farmhouse table used in lieu of a traditional coffee table. A deep chocolate-brown sofa and a cozy 25-year-old armchair upholstered in mossy-green velvet— the favorite lounging spot of Barney the Border Collie—provide cushy comfort.

The dining area owes its beguiling aura to a small rustic oak English table, one of Deborah's favorite pieces, which she has paired with an assortment of French chairs. Two of these have been reupholstered in floral linen, which she dyed using coffee to give it an aged appearance. The rusticity of an antique bench-turned-hanging rack contrasts with a midnight-blue wallpaper dotted with shimmering marigolds that sparkle by candlelight or when brushed by sunrays. Large scratches on the old oak floors are not hidden away but left untouched as precious reminders of the childhood days of the couple's now adult sons.

Old-fashioned romance fills the kitchen where there are always dried flowers, herbs and garlic from the adjacent garden. A self-proclaimed city homesteader and homemaker, Deborah enjoys spending many hours in the kitchen each day.

PAGES 46–47 Deborah has had the French armoire for over 40 years. It is made of solid oak and she finished it by layering light coats of brown, black and then blue paint. It's where she hangs dried flowers and displays her favorite antique transferware bowl, which holds seasonal treasures. On the Oushak rug, bought from M. Reyes Lifestyle on Instagram, stands a farmhouse-style table. This was originally used in the garden, where it acquired its weathered patina. Its height and size recall those of a library table.

ABOVE A narrow spare room has been made into a pantry with the help of an old pine English armoire, which provides safekeeping for fine wines and vintage table linens.

OPPOSITE Although designed for a bedroom, this classic dresser/chest of drawers from Ethan Allen is perfectly at home in the living room. As intended, it functions as storage while offering a staging area for an ever-changing display of objects. The green velvet armchair lends a subtle touch of faded glamour.

OPPOSITE In the dining room, rustic and refined textures and hues hold equal sway. The juxtaposition of materials and styles—simple cane chairs with classic upholstered ones, a weathered bucket and sparkling wallpaper, a delicate chandelier and a primitive shelf—creates visual poetry and highlights the room's earthy and romantic qualities.

RIGHT Deborah has achieved a harmonious blend of form and function by paying careful attention to the lines and materials of her furniture and accessories. The tables, one used for dining and the other for display, are united by their wooden finish. Two galvanized buckets, one filled with fluffy peonies and the other holding a small olive tree, create another visual echo. The chandelier and the small candelabra are both defined by their gentle curves.

PAGES 52 & 53 The kitchen is charming yet simple. Baskets and copper pots recall French country kitchens, while dried flowers and potted herbs bring home the English countryside.

"There's no dishwasher by choice," she notes. "The sink is perfect for washing large pots and the handcrafted brass faucet adds to the room's authenticity." A friend suggested mounting a vintage French door on the wall as an unusual shelf for her collection of copper pots, special gifts from David that she uses on a daily basis.

In the guest bedroom, red and green toiles create a fresh, garden-like effect. The master bedroom's hand-forged iron bed is a one-of-a-kind custom piece, made to look like heart-shaped butterfly wings. A nature lover, Deborah never fails to include flowers in her spaces. "I love decorating with floral branches. They bring in happiness. The orange trumpet stems on the nightstand are from the garden, and we watch the hummingbirds enjoy them through the kitchen window."

This little home isn't fancy or fussy or solemn, but it has a quality of integrity and friendliness that radiates from the natural beauty Deborah has created. "We are true romantics," she says, "and our little cottage hugs all those who enter."

"We are true romantics, and our little cottage hugs all those who enter."

OPPOSITE & LEFT Deborah likes to bring garden motifs and colors indoors. In the guest bedroom, French toile in varying hues brings a pastoral pattern to the curtains, pillow and bedspread. Furniture and accessories are carefully chosen and, in typical Deborah style, the rustic and the elegant both have a place. A delicate crystal sconce watches over a painted wooden stool, while a French table from the 1900s wears its original floral paintwork.

BELOW With its heart-shaped butterfly wings design, the bed seduced Deborah. "Butterflies bring a sense of calm," she says. "And they are believed to be a symbol of love. The bedroom is the perfect place to have both." Add luxurious silk and velvet bed linens, and you have all the elements for romance.

Artistic LICENSE

MOVING IS OFTEN A DAUNTING EXPERIENCE, ESPECIALLY WHEN IT INVOLVES HAVING TO SETTLE FOR A HOME THAT DOESN'T REALLY TUG AT YOUR HEARTSTRINGS. YET, BY OVERCOMING THE LIMITATIONS OF HER RENTED HOME IN CALIFORNIA, CREATIVE AND DESIGNER DORÉ CALLAWAY HAS PROVED THAT YOU CAN TAKE THE ARTIST OUT OF HER ELEMENT, BUT YOU CAN'T TAKE THE ART OUT OF THE ARTIST.

Creativity is in Doré's DNA. She learned at the feet of her paternal grandfather, Delbert H. Callaway, who was an art producer for Paramount Pictures and other studios in Hollywood. Doré would spend many hours at his weekend home in the desert, learning paint techniques from the man who created sets for John Wayne movies and *Gone with the Wind*. But when Doré had to find her own place to call home, she was faced with having to rent due to the sky-high prices of the California real estate market. "I knew this house wouldn't be my forever home, but it had some interesting features I could work with," Doré explains. "With its terracotta tiled roof, arched walkways and windows and private courtyard, it had a Spanish style fitting for Southern California." The spacious open floor plan, wood floors, high ceilings and large windows helped to guide her decision. "It felt like an artist's studio, a place I knew would inspire me. Living here would also allow me to simplify my lifestyle and design with pieces both beautiful and functional."

Doré is not new to the design world, either. Though she has worked as a graphic artist and as an interior designer of high-end model homes, she is also a talented artist.

ABOVE With a raw, weathered finish accentuated by a little white paint left in its crevices for added aging, the antique oak chest shows off one of Doré's many artistic skills. "It's a piece created out of necessity for elegant, functional storage," she says.

OPPOSITE When Doré acquired this early 1980s dining set, it was wearing its original dark stain. She sanded it down and applied a whitewashed finish to give it a fresh look and a European country style. "I love the lion-claw feet of the table," she says. "They add so much character."

OPPOSITE By removing its doors and drawers and refinishing it in her signature style, Doré transformed a former TV armoire into an elegant and useful storage piece. She uses it to display her collection of ironstone ceramics, plates, bowls, platters and favorite accessories.

RIGHT Doré has been collecting old candlesticks for many years. She favors metal pieces in varied heights and shapes for interesting tablescapes.

FAR RIGHT Stoneware crocks, canisters and confit pots are filled with rustic wooden kitchen utensils, including a selection of hand-carved spoons.

Her work includes mixed-media theater shadowboxes, hand-painted sign art, wirework creations, wood panel paintings and ornate birdhouses made from vintage frames and candlesticks. Doré is also the owner of Burlap Luxe, a European-inspired company specializing in decorative painting and dramatic restyling of vintage furniture. Although it was difficult to adjust to the limitations of renting, her love of weathered, salvaged and recast items is evident. "Having to make furniture fit in the spaces without any physical alterations to the rooms drove me to restrain myself," she says.

One of the first things Doré did was to paint the walls a soft flesh tone that gives the living room a very subtle warm glow.

LEFT "The kitchen needed some country charm," Doré notes. To achieve her desired look, she removed the upper cabinet doors and replaced the lower ones with dropcloth curtains. In lieu of an island, she uses a vintage French dresser/ chest of drawers that she white-washed with a damp rag to produce a weathered finish.

LEFT No furniture escapes the artist's touch. This refinished armoire bears Doré's signature aged look. However, she says, "I made sure to go lightly in order to show off its imperfections."

BELOW "The sideboard was a find in African mahogany, with a dark stain and an unsightly scratched finish," Doré recalls. "It would be an unwanted piece to so many, but not to me!" She once again worked her magical transformation on the piece. The mirror, another "ugly duckling," has morphed into a beauty in her skillful hands.

THIS PAGE The door leaning against the far wall holds a special place in Doré's heart because she salvaged it from her grandparents' home. Textured materials add tactile layers to the neutral palette: French linen on the sofa, dropcloth curtains, chairs upholstered in hemp and a handwoven twine and jute rug.

THIS PAGE Doré gave the old black iron bed frame a new look with a creamy hue, which she distressed for an aged vibe. A dropcloth bed skirt and comforter/duvet cover confer country charm, while floral pillows in muted shades inject a feminine touch. The antique trunk, a family heirloom, lends heft to the airy space.

OPPOSITE The guest room owes its romantic, ethereal mood to a variation of neutral hues, ranging from alabaster to bleached and many shades in between, with metal and stone accents. The bed is layered with linens and quilts in shades of cream and white that create a cocoon-like effect.

"Imperfections hold a special kind of romance for me."

Next, she worked the walls and wood floor color into her furnishings' raw and weathered finishes, giving them the appearance of having been bleached and silvered by the sun. "This was a good change, as it compelled me to work with the palette and not against it," Doré notes. She then proceeded to replace all the generic light fixtures with chandeliers and lanterns. This, and much more, is how Doré works to create her unmistakable signature style. "I often see romantic attributes in the unexpected. From music to objects that speak to my soul, the poetry in the pieces I design, a dark moody color or a paler one, the mix of natural woods with decaying stone garden urns, the list goes on," she says. She is most passionate about relaxed vintage and antiques, those

that show how much loved they once were. "I gravitate to pieces with cracks, chips and splits, and warped woods. Imperfections hold a special kind of romance for me."

Doré never backs away from a challenge. "With this home, it wasn't a question of thinking out of the box but of what could I do with the box? I made sure to feature statement pieces that would enhance yet not dwarf the rooms. It's all about accepting what you have to work with," she says. She opted to set favorite pieces throughout her home instead of grouping them in one larger space, thus allowing each to reveal their beauty and function efficiently. "My house is very natural. It's calming, spiritual and soothing—just the way I like it," she concludes. Her grandfather would surely approve.

CHAPTER 2
Modern Crush

Test of TIME

"I HAVE ALWAYS BEEN OBSESSED WITH THE QUIRKY QUEEN ANNE STYLE OF ARCHITECTURE," SAYS ART CURATOR AND DESIGNER MARIE SAMUELS. SO IT'S NOT SURPRISING THAT WHEN SHE SAW A "FOR SALE" SIGN IN FRONT OF A SIGNIFICANT TWO-AND-A-HALF-STORY, 1881 RAMBLING COTTAGE IN THE HISTORIC HILL DISTRICT OF NEWPORT, RHODE ISLAND, SHE FELT COMPELLED TO INVESTIGATE FURTHER.

Newport is famous for its Gilded Age mansions, which were once home to families such as the Vanderbilts, Wetmores and Astors, and for its upscale neighborhoods, like the one where the property that caught Marie's eye is located. The home's proximity to downtown and the beach only added to its appeal. Set within a spacious garden lot on a tree-lined street, the building itself was designed by Clarence Sumner Luce, one of the era's most esteemed architects, who set up a thriving practice here in Newport in the 1880s.

Upon entering the 140-year-old home, Marie observed the extent of the restoration that would be needed to repair the sagging ceilings and bowed walls. A complete remodel of the dated bathrooms and kitchen would also be required. On the plus side, she was pleased to see how well the home's 19th-century artistry had been preserved, including the hand-carved paneling, the stairway banister and the front door. She also loved the high ceilings, the scale of the windows and the amount of wall space on offer—a must for displaying the ever-growing collection of artworks she has acquired over the past 20 years.

Marie and her husband William bought the 4,800-square-foot/446-square-meter relic and turned to the contractor who had restored the couple's previous home.

ABOVE In the entry, minimal furnishings have a strong impact. A tall, sleek wooden table provides just the right amount of polish and glamour, but defers to the 19th-century architecture. Votives made of amethyst offer texture and color.

OPPOSITE An abundance of light from the original windows and a profusion of verdant plants and orchids denote a biophilic approach to interior design. The lush greenery gives the dining room a conservatory-like appearance that recalls the Victorian era. An organic quality unites the rattan table and bamboo deck chairs.

OPPOSITE & ABOVE The den features a large bay window that is characteristic of architecture from this period. The low-profile modern sofa, upholstered in buttery soft leather, is a favorite spot for relaxing. A trio of vintage terrazzo tables adds an artisanal touch. The curvy retro chair and a colorful abstract by Frank Stella put a contemporary spin on mid-century style.

RIGHT On one side of the den, a handmade oak console holds some of Marie's items and tomes, which she groups according to their significance and color values. Here, books and glass collectible objects in shades of aqua and blue share a water-related theme.

PAGES 70–71 The living room continues the modern and elegant yet approachable style and showcases the potential for contemporary pieces to bring personality to period homes. The curved bronze tables offset the straight-lined sofas. A painting by Belgian artist Karin Gielen and an original stained-glass window have an equally artful quality.

Once the extensive structural renovation work was complete, Marie set out to bring fresh life to the rooms. Though she appreciates the intricacy of the original hand-hewn details, she is not a fan of the dark finishes, exuberant ornamentation and somewhat fussy decor associated with the period. Instead, she favors a clean backdrop against which to showcase art and objects, a look that goes hand in hand with the simplicity of the Scandinavian interiors that she admires most. "Combining period architecture with modern furnishings creates an interesting mix that produces an energetic tension between old and new," she explains.

Marie began by painting the walls and ceilings a crisp shade of white that keeps the existing 19th-century design features present but prevents them from overwhelming the spaces.

ABOVE & OPPOSITE The original oak flooring running throughout the home has been sandblasted to reveal the honey-toned wood. It supplies a mellow foundation for a predominantly white palette that allows furnishings and artworks to shine. The gallery-like walls are an ideal backdrop for contemporary works. Though Marie has incorporated a few well-chosen antiques, such as this wing chair, she usually favors modern art and design. "I tend to buy things that I don't understand and have never seen before," she explains.

RIGHT These luminous, delicate "crystal balls" are sculptures by Laura Kramer. The two in the foreground are covered on the exterior with glass canes resembling barnacles, while the blue piece is made from vintage slag glass.

To further enhance the scheme, the original oak floors were sandblasted to reveal their pale beauty. Marie carefully balanced the authentic roots of the house with modern comfort and functionality. Each room is accentuated by contemporary pieces and a few antiques. The clean lines of the interiors extend from one space to the next, while a profusion of ferns and orchids honors the home's romantic history.

OPPOSITE During the remodel of the kitchen, a staircase to the upper floor was removed to enlarge the space. Stairs leading down to the basement were hidden beneath a trap door in the pine floor, which was salvaged from a 200-year-old church. Rattan vintage pendants illuminate the island, which functions as a grazing station.

LEFT The stairway's banister, latticework and original hand-carved wood panels were well preserved but in need of a refresh. Marie accomplished this with a few coats of Simply White by Benjamin Moore and a sisal carpet. A glass artwork, called *Floor Gems* by artist John Torreano, injects a modern note.

ABOVE The kitchen makeover was informed and guided by Marie's love of cooking and entertaining. The revamp includes new quartz counters, cabinetry with plenty of hidden storage and open shelves that keep everyday items visible and accessible. "It's my favorite room in the house," Marie says.

THIS PAGE The master bedroom gets its cozy, island vibe from a new pine bed with a woven headboard, a striped pillow and a luxurious vintage Moroccan blanket with hundreds of mirrored sequins (a wedding gift). A textural sisal rug and a scalloped rattan basket add to the tactile, relaxed feel of the space.

OPPOSITE Marie has carefully curated her home as a playful yet sophisticated space through considered choices of colors, furnishings and accessories. Here, pink vintage linen reveals the romantic side of a classic armchair, while the timeless green-and-white cabana stripes of the pillow hint at poolside cocktails and endless summer days.

Under Marie and William's considerate stewardship, this historic 140-year-old home has stood the test of time. Its new owners have paid homage to its beautiful, original craftsmanship and retained the one-of-a-kind architectural parameters that came with the property. The result is a uniquely sleek, chic and exciting interior, which works as well for modern-day living as it did in Newport's Gilded Age.

State of BLISS

KELLEY MOTSCHENBACHER'S WILD LOVE AFFAIR WITH INTERIOR DESIGN HAS LED HER ON A PASSIONATE JOURNEY THAT, SHE SAYS, "WAS CRAZY AND SOMETIMES DAUNTING, ESPECIALLY WHEN I OWNED TOO MANY DIFFERENT PROPERTIES SIMULTANEOUSLY." YET, WITH ITS INCREDIBLE PANORAMIC VISTA OVER DOWNTOWN LOS ANGELES, THIS 27TH-FLOOR APARTMENT IN A 30-STORY BUILDING PROVED TO BE IRRESISTIBLE FOR THE INTREPID DESIGNER AND HER CREATIVE BRAIN WENT INTO OVERDRIVE. "THE INTERIOR WAS A PERFECTLY BLANK CANVAS AND THE VIEWS OF THE CITY SKYLINE WERE BREATHTAKING."

The idea of living in "a high-rise, supercharged urban environment" appealed to Kelley and her husband Greg, and not just because of the rich history of their new neighborhood and its amazing local food scene. "When we moved in, I was involved with several design and building projects and Greg was working on a number of commercial construction developments downtown," she explains. "For the first time in his career, he was able to walk to his office near the iconic Los Angeles Central Library."

Although moving into the brand-new building was "a great experience," Kelley says there were a few challenges to contend with when she and Greg first arrived. "For one thing, the apartment has lots of floor-to-ceiling windows and very few walls, which made it tricky to find places for our existing furniture. We managed it in the end, though it necessitated cutting some pieces down to fit." Undeterred, Kelley embraced the limitations of the space and kept rearranging the furnishings until everything felt good. Some of the rooms have been assigned new roles, too.

ABOVE In keeping with the modernity of her home's architecture and of the adjoining kitchen, Kelley opted to go with a mid-century Tulip dining table by Eero Saarinen from Design Within Reach. The teak chairs, while simple in silhouette, make a textural statement with their intricately woven leather seats.

OPPOSITE Though streamlined, the kitchen is big on style and function. The island works as a breakfast bar while providing workspace for meal preparation. Slipcovers make ordinary stools look appropriately chic. For additional storage, a metal shelving unit was painted white to work with the neutral color scheme.

THIS PAGE With its mix of cool, modern accents and rustic antique furnishings, the living room showcases Kelley's affinity for contemporary designs and her love of vintage. Threads of different eras and aesthetics are woven together to create a characterful space. The blue antique cabinet is from Prize in Kansas City, Missouri.

"I generally lean into natural tones, but I also love strong colors, whites and textures. I've never met a basket, a piece of ticking or an odd bit of pottery I didn't love."

BELOW Originally bought for storage, this sleek stainless-steel sideboard turned out to be just the right surface on which to place the television. When not in use, the screen becomes one of several black accents that contribute depth and definition to the room.

She decided to use what was meant to be the master bedroom as her home office, setting a modern desk in the niche where the bed was intended to go. "Adding comfy big chairs, a soft rug and lots of storage baskets created a den-like space." The second bedroom, meanwhile, has been promoted to master bedroom status.

"History is my inspiration," Kelley says. "All the designers and creatives I admire greatly are very original and focused. Watching people do what they love and doing it incredibly well moves me." Details, interesting color combinations, art and nature also influence her design philosophy. The kaleidoscopic views and the modernity of the space also guided her choices for her new home, in which she aspired to set a curated, romantic country mood underscored with modern influences. She has achieved this via the opposition of rustic antiques with contemporary items in a way that lets everything shine.

"I used many iconic pieces from both genres—it keeps the look interesting, fresh and cozy," Kelley says.

OPPOSITE In the entry, a large oil painting from a flea market presides over an old Asian elm bench topped with a Navajo rug from Mexico and pillows sewn from mismatched vintage fabrics. These blue-and-white accents hint at the colors to be found within the home.

OPPOSITE "We decided to use the main bedroom as an office because of its size," Kelley explains. "I used old scaffold planks for the shelving, bought a minimal desk and brought in a dining-room chair, which works well in the space." The oversized sisal rug with its modern stripes complements the contemporary look. A stack of big rattan baskets provides ample storage.

RIGHT Kelley had an old English armchair reupholstered in sackcloth. "The other seat is a large chair-and-a-half," she says. "It's so comfy and perfect for reading or a coffee break." Unique pieces like the antique English bamboo side table and the rattan ottoman bring in a vintage flavor.

One of her favorite combinations can be found in the living room, where an 1850s cupboard in its original blue paint has teamed up with a perfectly proportioned Eames chair in buttery leather. "I generally lean into natural tones, but I also love strong colors, whites and textures. I've never met a basket, a piece of ticking or an odd bit of pottery I didn't love."

Though she prefers authentic furnishings, Kelley has a pragmatic approach to decorating. "Sometimes it's necessary to buy things that may not have the quality you love and mix in the "real" stuff—you just have to make them work together."

RIGHT Though a few inches had to be cut off the base of this black RH shelving unit to fit it in the apartment, it was worth the trouble. It offers much-needed storage in the office and, along with the vintage signs, adds a graphic punch.

LEFT "With the exception of the mid-19th-century embellished folk art cupboard, everything in the master bedroom is new," says Kelley. She loves living in a modern space, but still managed to incorporate this unusual piece from the 1850s. "It works and they look great together."

RIGHT Kelley envisioned a transitional feel in the bedroom. "The woven platform bed from Williams-Sonoma was the most expensive piece, but the other items were off-the-shelf and easy to find." Though the overall look is modern, assorted block-print pillows and an Indian wool throw share a commonality of textures and colors.

RIGHT Though small, the guest bathroom has plenty of sophistication thanks to its black-and-white scheme. Framed photos convey a touch of artistry, while towels are kept handy on a hotel-style rack. A French portmanteau fashioned from an old vine strikes a whimsical rustic note.

However, it is still a good idea to be selective and look for pieces that you will treasure for years to come, she advises. "Always buy vintage over new, if you can."

It was only a matter of time before Kelly's pursuit of beautiful home decor and her love of design would lead to a new venture. In 2021 she opened Blu Canoe, which she describes as "a creative little business in a small space on tiny Balboa Island," where she offers full design services, vintage furniture and distinctive garden items. For most, bliss is a state of mind, but for Kelley it's something much more tangible.

CHAPTER 3
Love Stories

True DEVOTION

ALTHOUGH THEIR FLORIDA HOME IS NOT OLD,
ITS BESPOKE INTERIOR IS A TESTAMENT TO
ISABELLA AND ROBERT NELSON'S AFFECTION
FOR ALL THINGS ROMANTIC, WITH UNDERTONES
THAT HONOR THE PAST AND THE PRESENT.
ISABELLA'S SOFT AND FEMININE TOUCHES
ILLUMINATE EVERY SPACE, WHILE ROBERT'S
DISCERNING EYE FOR ITEMS WITH AGE AND
CHARACTER IS THE PERFECT COUNTERPOINT.
IF THERE EVER WAS A DREAM DECORATING
TEAM, LOOK NO FURTHER, THEY ARE IT.

The home's classic Mediterranean style caught their
attention and its proximity to Sarasota's historic downtown
district and local beaches sealed the deal. "It felt like a
private oasis and offered endless opportunities to create
the perfect place that we could call home," Isabella says.
And though the 3,300-square-foot/307-square-meter
interior was somewhat lacking in architectural character,
Isabella and Robert knew this could be quickly remedied.
They began by installing no fewer than 18 chandeliers and
other antique elements throughout the space. "Our vision
was for an environment that captured the romance of a
fine, ornate yet comfortable home—think classic French
and Italianate overtones softened by traditional American
pieces," says Isabella. "We love white marble, gilded
finishes, carved wood and opulent lighting juxtaposed with
farmhouse tables and Chesterfield sofas. We also like to
display contemporary art alongside traditional elements
to present a modern take on the Paris apartment vibe."

As the owners of Bon Bon Vintage, one of the most
exquisite shops in Sarasota, Isabella and Robert have
traveled far and wide to source unique finds for the store.

OPPOSITE An elegant Italian leather sofa teamed
with a distressed mango wood table, a cabinet
constructed from reclaimed planks, a 19th-century
Egyptian door and a Turkish rug define Isabella and
Robert's mix of refined and low-key glamour.

ABOVE The foyer introduces the home's romantic
influences and neutral palette—the walls in every
room are painted in Egret White by Sherwin-Williams.
The classic French mirror and candelabra evoke the
look of a sophisticated European home.

THIS PAGE Though the kitchen, living and dining areas are open to one another and have a shared palette of colors and textures, each space is clearly defined by its furnishings. Chandeliers and chairs with an old-world flair balance the modernity of the island, while a French bench and low chairs soften the heft of the dining table.

This also gives them plenty of opportunities to furnish their home with antiques and vintage pieces—think crystal chandeliers, intricately carved furniture and stately mirrors that add a perfect touch of gravitas and history to every room. Although these treasures take center stage, the couple also likes to include current items, from tableware to bed linen, all with simple elegance and European flair.

In both the store and their home, Isabella's great eye and keen design sense come into play harmoniously alongside Robert's masculine input. Texture is an important consideration for them both. "Every room can use a bit of glitter and gleam, whether from mirrors, metals or lacquered pieces. Shimmering surfaces reflect light and contribute to a romantic effect," says Isabella. "But one must also keep in mind the importance of soft, tactile materials as essential components of a lush and sensual environment."

The result is rooms that exude a low-key glamour underscored by an alluring comfort—an inviting combination that defines their personality and charm.

ABOVE Antique slipcovered wing chairs, an Italian gilt wood sconce and a pair of floor-to-ceiling bookcases with intricate carvings temper the modernity of a new table with a glass top and a gold-leafed metal base. A trip to Charleston, South Carolina inspired the collection of blue-and-white ginger jars.

OPPOSITE In keeping with the European theme, the library is home to a Louis XV desk and a vintage Italianate chair with a gilded metal frame and velvet upholstery. A pair of new lamps sports unusual metal shades. The frame of the ornate reproduction mirror was lacquered with white to match the desk.

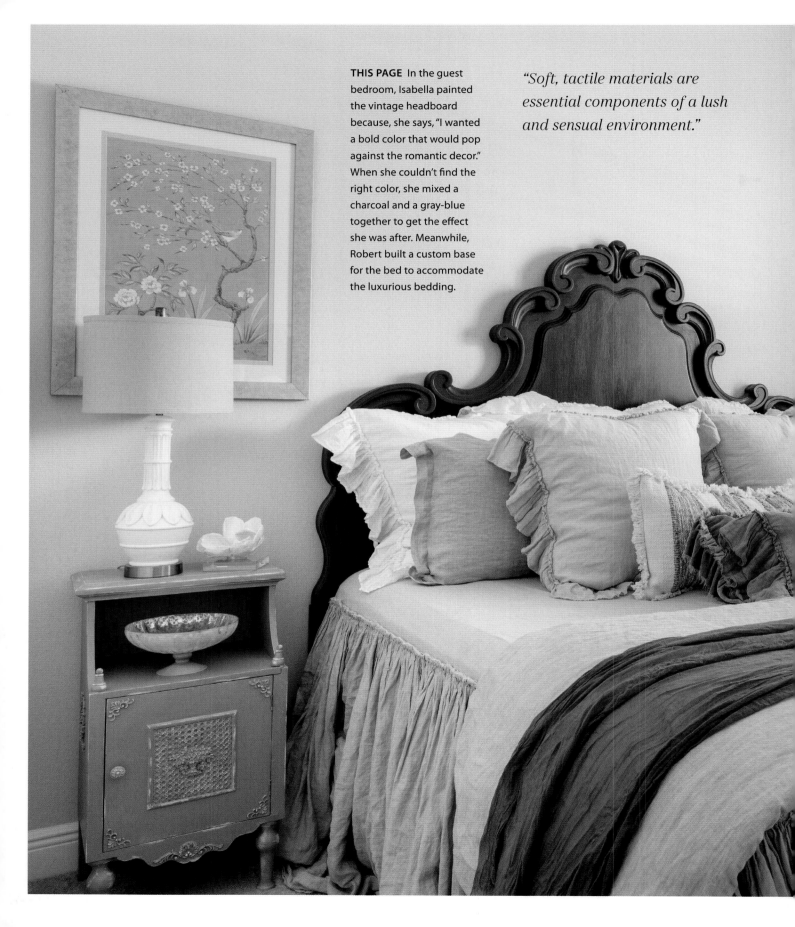

THIS PAGE In the guest bedroom, Isabella painted the vintage headboard because, she says, "I wanted a bold color that would pop against the romantic decor." When she couldn't find the right color, she mixed a charcoal and a gray-blue together to get the effect she was after. Meanwhile, Robert built a custom base for the bed to accommodate the luxurious bedding.

"Soft, tactile materials are essential components of a lush and sensual environment."

ABOVE Isabella loves hearts and is always on the hunt for more pieces to add to her growing collection. The color and motif of the framed chinoiserie wallpaper continues the romantic vibe.

Isabella credits much of their design inspiration from visiting grand homes, historic estates and landmark hotels in American cities such as Seattle, Napa, New York, Charleston, Savannah, New Orleans and Miami. Echoes of their travels can be found in every room of the home. For instance, the dining room, Robert's favorite space, is decorated in a way that reflects the sultry romance of the Deep South: wooden shutters, palm trees and antique urns frame a rustic table capped with an antique Spanish crystal chandelier. Meanwhile, Isabella has a soft spot for the master bedroom with its ample, curvaceous bed dressed in a voluptuous gathering of luxurious linens, silk velvets and oversized pillows.

"The hardest part for us both is deciding what to bring in," Isabella confesses. "The never-ending series of options that present themselves by way of the store only makes things worse!" And, adding to the dilemma, she says, "There is no permanence in decor. Designing a harmonious and personal space is an evolutionary process. It is that quest for perfection that drives endless acquisitions and makes the whole process enjoyable." Echoing that ethos, Isabella and Robert's home exemplifies their true devotion to romantic bliss.

OPPOSITE & RIGHT Antique doors from Malta add texture and warmth to the master bedroom's white scheme. The family's Papillon pups—Leonardo da Vinci, Lorenzo de Medici and Lilian Seraphina—appreciate the luxurious velvet and linen Bella Notte bedding. A gilded tray and lamp add a subtle Midas touch to the elegant decor.

BELOW Isabella couldn't wait to replace the basic lights in the bathroom with these flower sconces made with crystal and soft pink glass. Antique frames that were stashed away for two years before the couple bought their home have been fitted with beveled mirrors. Oversized mercury urns and new cabinet handles amp up the glamour quotient.

Lasting
IMPRESSIONS

DECORATING AFICIONADOS FIND INSPIRATION TO CREATE THEIR FAVORITE ENVIRONMENT FROM MANY AND VARIED SOURCES. BUT FOR ROMANTIC SOULS, IT ALWAYS SEEMS TO COME DOWN TO THEIR CHOICE OF COLORS, STYLE AND ERA, AND JANET SOLOMON'S COTTAGE IN SAN CLEMENTE, CALIFORNIA IS A PERFECT EXAMPLE.

Janet has always been in love with the coast and for as long as she can remember her fondness for the ocean has been the main influence for her palette of soft blues and lavenders, flaxen whites and bleached linens. But a trip to France (the first of many) kick-started her home's fresh look and put a new spin on her beachside theme. "I fell under the spell of the culture of France, and it changed my style completely," she says. "I adore anything old and worn. The more so, the better."

Their yearly voyages took Janet and her husband Larry mainly to Paris and the Provençal countryside, where they bought books, artworks, accessories and even furniture, including a pair of crown-motif chairs. "It's such a thrill when you discover a great piece," Janet says, recalling early mornings spent wandering through flea markets. "You never know what you will find. You fall in love with it and simply must have it." And just like that, the 1960s beach house that she and Larry have shared for more than 30 years, where they raised their three children, began to take on a new personality and a European spirit.

Though Janet kept some of the coastal hues she loved, she softened the palette and brought in misty blues, pale grays and watercolor-like greens and lavenders.

OPPOSITE Dripping with crystals that have turned a pale lavender over the years, a vintage chandelier presides over a newer table. The black chair, handed down from Larry's grandparents, was reupholstered with an off-white damask. Vintage chairs have been given a new life with linen slipcovers.

ABOVE The antique mirror's shape makes a pleasing counterpoint to the simple, narrow side table. The plank-and-beam ceiling and open kitchen have a cottage feel that balances the elegance of the space.

"My former decor was more beachy and cottagey, whereas I wanted to make our home feel as if we lived on the coast of France, so I removed anything that didn't fit that dream," Janet says. "I bought French books, shell art and much more. My favorite find was from a flea market in Paris. It's an old, tattered oil painting of the ocean and a boat, which is now in our living room. To this day, it still makes my heart sing."

The kitchen underwent a few changes in tune with Janet's love of European interiors. "The cabinets are original to the house, and I still prefer them over new," she says. "But since the doors no longer closed, we removed them, which made the space more compatible with the style of kitchens you often see in rural France, plus they work much better with our lifestyle. We also replaced the dark gray-blue Formica countertops with stone tiles."

ABOVE Open cabinets filled with collected items give the remodeled kitchen a European flair. The stone counter functions as a staging area for preparing food and as a place for everyday meals. Plus, it makes a convenient buffet or bar when the couple entertains dinner guests. "It's very versatile and works for whatever we are doing," Janet says.

RIGHT Janet's daughter Noel is an artist who creates one-of-a-kind pieces using French paper. Though blooms are the hallmark of Noel's work, she and Janet also make pretty paper cones that resemble those given at weddings and baptisms in France. Theirs are filled with little surprises and presented to guests as a parting gift.

THIS PAGE A pine farm table made from floor planks hails from a brewery in England. It holds favorite items and old French books, which Janet favors for their texture and because, she says, "Although I can't interpret the meaning of the words, I know it's there." Some of Noel's dramatic masterpieces fit right in with the decor.

LEFT The living room's subtle palette forms a soothing background for the unique furnishings. The small blue table once belonged to the Hotel Napoleon in Paris. The armoire wears its original black paint, as does the coffee table. Janet favors the contrast of the dark pieces with the lighter ones. The large oil portrait was found in New York and the smaller painting on the table at a Paris flea market.

BELOW The trunks and hatbox are from Goyard, a French luggage maker that has been at the same Paris location since 1834. The waterproof canvas features a dotted chevron pattern in which the address of the store is artistically hidden.

In the dining room, the couple took down the existing nautical silver-toned light fixture and, in its place, installed a 100-year-old chandelier, which adds a touch of drama and is a focal point of the decoration. "We found the chandelier at a flea market—it came from a church in Italy and was made for candles, but I had it wired so that we could hang it over our table," Janet says. "Rainbows dance on the walls in the afternoon when the light reflects off the crystals just right and some of those crystals are now turning a shade of lavender from exposure to the sun. I love that only time can create that change and that one must slow down enough to observe this process taking place."

ABOVE These wings were made from old hemp fabric and purchased at a flea market in Paris by one of Janet's friends. They would have been sewn by hand for children to wear in a Christmas procession and are prized collectibles in France.

LEFT & OPPOSITE The English hutch/dresser, a coveted family piece, was a gift to Janet from her mother. The desk is newer, but both pieces anchor the room and contribute to its sophistication. Janet's fondness for old French paintings is evident here: an oil portrait unites with the darker tones in the decor, while a small painting reflects the softer hues. Found in a Los Angeles shop specializing in unique vintage furniture, the linen-upholstered armchair shows off its original French blue paint and the carving of its frame.

THIS PAGE Janet chose the painting over the bed for its colors. "It is perfect for my palette," she notes. She brought back the bed throw—dyed a lavender hue—from a trip to the South of France. The silk-cushioned French bench is a lucky flea-market find, as is the chair with its distinctively carved V-shaped back and white leather upholstery.

ABOVE Janet delights in composing little vignettes. Gleaming silver, lustrous pearls, silky ribbons and fresh lilacs are discreet but romantic touches appropriately fitting to the bedroom's calming palette and understated feminine decor.

"It's such a thrill when you discover a great piece."

Janet is always on the hunt for rare pieces. "Like the tides, my home decor ebbs and flows," she says. "Although nothing stays the same, love is a constant." And when asked if there is a particular item she'd love to find, Janet doesn't hesitate. "I dream of having an old French birdcage in the courtyard with a pair of white doves living inside. They represent peace and I love the sound they make." Isn't that romantic?

LEFT Restored and painted, the once sad little cottage now stands like a pearl within the shell garden. Wood and rattan furniture brings a touch of warmth to the white exterior. The deck is a lovely spot for a morning coffee or evening glass of wine. White flowers and mossy concrete hearts have a romantic significance.

OPPOSITE A baroque mirror brings a vintage vibe to the living room. The reflective surface adds dimension, a must for a small space. Despite its size, the blush armchair fits comfortably in the room. A concrete stool functions as a side table. The graphic canvas artwork draws the eye upward.

Terms of
ENDEARMENT

DESPITE ITS CONDITION, THE MOMENT I SAW THIS 100-YEAR-OLD COTTAGE IN FLORIDA I HAD A FEELING THAT IN FRENCH WOULD BE KNOWN AS A *COUP DE COEUR* (AN INSTANT CRUSH). THE WORDS OF THE WRITER VIRGINIA WOOLF CAME TO MIND INSTANTLY: "I FEEL SO INTENSELY THE DELIGHTS OF SHUTTING ONESELF UP IN A LITTLE WORLD OF ONE'S OWN, WITH PICTURES AND MUSIC AND EVERYTHING BEAUTIFUL." THIS IS THE VERY EMBODIMENT OF WHAT HOME MEANS TO ME, AND I KNEW I COULD ACHIEVE IT HERE.

The cottage was dark, damp and gloomy, yet there was no doubt in my heart that this tiny house was meant for me. I bought the ugly little duckling that nobody wanted. From the outside, it was already clear that the property needed a lot of work. But even the crumbling roof, mildewed siding, broken windows and collapsed deck didn't foretell the even worse condition of the interior. It was quite simply uninhabitable.

On the plus side, the layout was appealing, the rooms were bright and I loved the charming arched doorways. Rather than feeling cramped, the space felt like a cocoon. I have always had a particular affinity for small dwellings, and with its modest footprint of 640 square feet/ 60 square meters, this historic shack gave me a new vision for an idyllic lifestyle in which aesthetics and functionality would play equal roles.

THIS PAGE A white palette calls for hints of color and texture to avoid looking sterile. Here, rosy hues come from the palest blush of the chair, a woman's portrait, a whimsical sheep and several accessories. Woolly throws, a faux hide and small rattan and wood tables bring in the much-needed tactile element.

ABOVE LEFT & RIGHT The union of a vintage chair and mirror with a modern faux fireplace and stool brings both styles together in harmony. This design philosophy allows each element to shine while providing a dynamic balance. Metallic accents, such as the silver pot and bejeweled horseshoe on this stack of books, always bring a room to life.

OPPOSITE A small hallway between the kitchen and bedroom offers just enough room for a new buffet with a vintage feel. The mirror helps make the area appear larger and creates a smooth transition from one space to the next. The kitchen cart in the foreground provides extra storage for decorative and useful items.

Once the extensive remodeling was completed, the house was ready for decorating. I love many styles and all my previous homes went through a number of different phases over the years as my tastes evolved. It's part of the creative process for me—probably a side effect of my work as an interiors stylist. However, whatever look I choose to create, my spaces have always shared a romantic mood underscored by femininity, a little glamour and hints of whimsy. More than anything, it has always been the well-used and much-loved family heirlooms that helped me to form an emotional bond with the place where I live. These are the things that make a house a home.

Though I have remained faithful to my inner romantic, this time around I chose to update the look by including a few nods to current design styles.

LEFT Though the size of my kitchen is sufficient, its shape is long and narrow. To best utilize the available space, I kept the existing lower cabinets and added shelves wherever possible. Staying with a black-and-white palette lends the room a little sophistication while adding a narrow table provides workspace and room for meals.

ABOVE Different in style but similar in tone, the items on the shelves and the counter keep the color scheme constant. Small appliances fit nicely in their allotted space, while vintage and new canisters provide pretty storage. A chicken-wire heart, a flower-filled basket and a few candles add to the quietly romantic undertones of my little cottage.

I have brought these more modern pieces into the fold, making optimal use of the space and paying close attention to scale. In the living room, a streamlined contemporary sofa balances the large baroque mirror, while a vintage chair offsets the 21st-century feel of the faux fireplace and clear Lucite side table.

I found that the key to keeping the somewhat eclectic style cohesive was to stay within an intentional color palette. I've always loved the gentle simplicity of white and soft rosy hues. The white-on-white scheme becomes luminescent when graced by the sunlight, with the blush accents imparting a tender fragility.

OPPOSITE Even when space is at premium, your home can be both functional and stylish. My office benefits from vertical storage—this bookshelf holds more than its intended function and also keeps things within reach. The crystal-clear Lucite chair is ideal because it appears to simply vanish.

LEFT The compact bathroom welcomes old and new: a curvy vintage mirror with a gold frame above a modern vanity. The glass basin imparts a spa vibe. The dark finish on the light fixture ties in with the streamlined shelf and towel bar.

ABOVE A space-saving corner table with round metal trays is a clever solution for keeping everyday necessities and small decorative items handy.

LEFT Why hide away your necklaces, rings and bracelets, whether new or vintage, when they can be put on display? I love how they become part of the decor and enhance the romantic aura of a room.

BELOW & RIGHT The slipcover on this headboard can be substituted for a pink or pale blue one for a quick and easy decorative refresh. A new black dresser/chest of drawers accentuates the soft palette, while a Lucite chair keeps the space from looking crowded. The antique crystal chandelier, mirror and portrait have a timeless beauty.

"I've always loved the gentle simplicity of white and soft rosy hues."

In the end, it's the life that happens inside a home that adds the color. Another tip is to allow for blank wall space to promote breathing room and prevent visual chaos, especially in a small interior. That same design ethos follows in the bedroom, office and bathroom. It's an effortless and easily attainable look that doesn't require lavish financial resources.

At the time of writing, I have only been in my home for a little over a year, so I am confident that it will continue to evolve over time. Although it's far from being spectacular or flawless, it is meaningful and personal. Whenever I am here, I unequivocally and intensely feel the delights of shutting myself up in my own little world.

CHAPTER 4
Classic Vibes

OPPOSITE The massive, original lava rock fireplace is the focal point of the great room. "It has remained even after we painted everything white," says Valerie. "Although its rustic charm was an asset, it did need a bit of romancing—hence the pink garden gate and an array of candlesticks. Everything was so brown when we moved in, I needed to add a rosy touch!"

ABOVE Outfitted with an old barn door, a chicken nesting box, a sink-turned-table, an antique bench and wicker chairs with handmade vintage ticking cushions, even the cozy outdoor space wears Valerie's signature romantic country style.

Countryside ROMANCE

WHEN VALERIE AND MIKE MADEIRA DECIDED TO BUY A HOME IN THE CHARMING TOWN OF SANTA YNEZ, CALIFORNIA, THEY SOON FOUND JUST WHAT THEY WERE LOOKING FOR. IN FACT, THIS HOUSE WAS THE VERY FIRST PROPERTY THEY VISITED AND IT IS ONLY A FEW BLOCKS AWAY FROM VALERIE'S QUAINT LITTLE ANTIQUES BOUTIQUE, VALERIE'S VINTAGE & SUPPLY CO. "WHEN WE WALKED THROUGH THE FRONT DOOR, I KNEW IT WAS THE RIGHT HOUSE!" SHE EXCLAIMS.

Not only was the location perfect but the home also offered more than enough space to accommodate visiting family and friends, with four bedrooms and two bathrooms. With a footprint of 2,700 square feet/250 square meters, there would also be plenty of room for the home's other full-time resident—Boscoe, the lovable five-year-old English Bulldog.

What first caught Valerie's attention when she stepped inside was the great room. "The open space stole my heart," she says. "It had soaring ceilings and the kitchen was brand new, and it all tied together with the dining and living room." The only drawback to this impressive space was purely cosmetic, and Valerie was prepared to compromise. "The walls were clad in brown wood paneling, which I didn't like but my husband and kids loved.

I decided to live with the existing decor for a few years before carrying out my grand scheme of changing it all."

Fast forward to 2021, when Valerie put her plan into action. "My son AJ was painting houses at the time, so I asked him to paint everything white," Valerie recalls. "His crew worked nonstop, filling all the paneling with 60 tubes of caulking and masking everything off, and within a couple of days everything was white." Though she is known for being quick when it comes to decorating decisions, she admits that defining each area of the voluminous space was her biggest challenge.

ABOVE A table base topped with an old door functions as a desk in the living room. Behind it, European shutters contribute another layer of texture. A rusty old metal basket and a small cast-iron urn create a distinctive tablescape.

RIGHT A former apothecary cabinet wearing its original paintwork was a fortuitous find. Its size and design turned out to be the perfect piece to function as a sideboard. A multitude of drawers offers convenient storage, while the upper portion becomes a stage for collections of frames, urns and glass seltzer bottles.

PAGE 127 A weathered cabinet combines style with function in the dining room. Its antique quality pairs well with the European pine table and the vintage zinc chandelier. Though they are not old, Valerie chose the chairs for the texture and color of the woven grass. Garden planters, like this Medici urn with its pretty scroll handles, are high on Valerie's list of prized collectibles.

RIGHT Despite the size of the great room, Valerie was able to create a cozy living area furnished with comfort and easy care in mind—a must with Roscoe the dog and her grandchildren to consider. The sofa, slipcovered with painter's cloths, beadboard trunk and well-worn rug are all impervious to possible mishaps. The white chandelier tempers the room's height without drawing attention to it.

"The ceilings are so tall that I needed to balance it all with a taller piece in the dining room, make the living room warm and cozy and create a play area for the grandkids."

"The ceilings are so tall that I needed to balance it all with a taller piece in the dining room, make the living room warm and cozy and create a play area for the grandkids," she explains. But when all was said and done, painting that great room white, rearranging the furniture and hanging some architectural pieces and old signs changed the dynamic of the space. "Now, every time I walk through my front door I feel at peace and fall in love with this place all over again. It's where memories are made, the boys hang out and the grandkids run around. It's our home!"

Valerie's mom had an antiques store when she was growing up, so it's no surprise that she would follow in her footsteps. "Her style was much more eclectic than mine, but she always had a great eye for French finds, cast-iron urns and garden statues.

OPPOSITE The kitchen had been updated prior to the couple buying the home, but Valerie was quick to put her stamp on the space. "I wanted to include something architectural to frame the window and these columns did the trick," she says. The rustic wooden signage brings a graphic element to the scheme.

ABOVE An existing recessed window with a wooden shelf makes an ideal showcase for glassware. Valerie is an avid collector of glass bottles in different shapes and sizes. "I love green bottles," she explains. "But they can't just be any green bottle. They must have an interesting shape, not a perfect one, and allow just enough natural light to pass through them."

RIGHT Large and small collectibles—from artworks to urns and more—can be seen lovingly displayed in every room. Here, set on rustic wood cutting boards, silver-topped glass salt, pepper and sugar shakers hold a variety of ingredients. Porcelainware adds luster to this simple but charming group of everyday objects.

OPPOSITE This spacious room serves as an office and as a studio where Valerie has set up an area to photograph smaller items and artworks from her shop to feature on her website. The barn door and picnic table provide the perfect backdrop for styling vintage and rustic garden pieces.

ABOVE "I am always drawn to antique black books," says Valerie of the volumes in this cabinet. "I started out collecting Bibles and moved on to dictionaries and encyclopedias and old photo albums, but they must be black." An eye-catching leopard-print chair and patinaed metal trunk add to the eclectic atmosphere.

I tend to gravitate toward the same," Valerie explains. "My store and my home both reflect that. I can't resist a leopard-print chair or a beautiful urn or chandelier." It only makes sense that Valerie would do most of her shopping in her own shop. "My number one rule is: If it doesn't sell, how will it look in my home? Sometimes I'll purchase something to put in the store and it ends up going home with me a few days later. Once I find a piece I love, I'm pretty content."

Though the Madeiras' home is already filled with meaningful items, Valerie is still on the lookout for artworks to hang on the walls, especially those that depict farm animals, flowers, books and, of course, her favorite breed of dog. "If I find a great antique Bulldog statue, I always buy it. I already know where it's going to land in my home."

THIS PAGE With its antique desk, girandole and chandelier, a sculptural 1920s wall sconce and handmade toile de Jouy pillows, the master bedroom shows off Valerie's flair for French antiques. True to her love of leopard fabrics, an animal-print chair—the twin to the one in the office (see page 133)—has been given a spot in this room, while a faux hide creates a layered effect.

Written
IN STONE

WITH ITS FIELDS OF PURPLE LAVENDER AND GOLDEN SUNFLOWERS, TOWERING CYPRESS TREES AND COLORFUL OPEN-AIR MARKETS, THE SOUTH OF FRANCE HAS LONG BEEN THE PLACE OF CHOICE FOR THOSE LONGING TO RECONNECT WITH NATURE AND A PEACEFUL LIFESTYLE. FOR SYLVIE SOMMER, WHO WAS BORN IN THE COUNTRYSIDE NEAR THE CITY OF AVIGNON, IT WAS ALSO A PLACE WHERE SHE COULD GO BACK TO HER ROOTS.

After living in London for more than 30 years, Sylvie decided to trade the hustle and bustle of big-city living for the serenity of village life in the French countryside. She envisioned a charming cottage with cozy rooms, a country kitchen and a large hearth. But instead, much to her surprise, she fell in love with an abandoned 200-year-old farmhouse constructed from local limestone with a typical Provençal terracotta roof. It was clear that the building was in need of major improvements. "The house had running water and electricity but lacked a kitchen or any other livable rooms—put simply, it was uninhabitable," Sylvie recalls. The news was not all bad, however. "The structure was sound and the setting idyllic," she explains, adding that the spacious, albeit unkempt garden also played a role in her decision. "Somehow I knew it was the right place for me."

Trusting her instincts, Sylvie created her dream home one room at a time. While preserving the original architectural details, including massive beams and wood plank ceilings, she transformed the spacious central part of the home into a combined living, dining and music room.

ABOVE Sylvie used two separate cabinets to create one piece of furniture by stacking them together. The upper tier acts as a library for vintage books, while the lower one provides elegant storage for mundane items—these are concealed behind chicken-wire panels lined with curtains.

OPPOSITE The Provençal dining table and chairs are typical of the region's classic furnishings. Displayed on the sideboard, a collection of *soupières* (soup tureens) attests to Sylvie's fondness for shapely dishes. Curated artworks in muted tones create a discreet gallery wall.

FAR LEFT A trio of decorative balls in a variety of materials—distressed rattan, scripted paper and tiny shells—are set on silver stands in a textural vignette.

LEFT Sentimental mementos, including hearts, a mercury vase and a silver box inscribed with "*amour*," are displayed atop an old table with a painterly, weathered finish.

BELOW Sylvie designed her limestone fireplace with inspiration from others she has seen in Provence. Though imposing, its simple form has an elegant look. A vintage table, chair and sofa create an intimate setting, while kilim rugs in rosy hues enliven the neutral palette.

This space now has a large wood-burning fireplace and a new graceful, airy spiral staircase leading to a mezzanine that would become the loft-style master suite. Off to one side of the open living area, she carved out space for a kitchen while dedicating the opposite side of the great room to a private guest bedroom and bath, ideal for hosting friends or for when her grown-up sons come to stay.

When it came to decorating, Sylvie let loose her passion for scouring local flea markets, antique fairs and *vide greniers* (yard sales). These weekly seasonal adventures are as much part of her lifestyle as croissants and coffee.

OPPOSITE Preserving the original architectural details, including beams and wood plank ceilings, was important to Sylvie. To maximize and direct natural light inside the house, she added a gracefully curved see-through spiral staircase and a half-wall of metal mesh on the new mezzanine where the master bedroom and bathroom are now located.

ABOVE In the kitchen, Sylvie integrated a fresh look with older elements. A curved marble backsplash behind the sink complements the stone countertops, farmhouse sink and subtle heart-themed accents. The hood of the stove/cooker has a handy metal shelf for keeping pots of fresh herbs within easy reach.

OPPOSITE When Sylvie began taking music lessons as a child, her parents purchased this 1911 grand piano. Over the years, it has followed Sylvie from house to house and now shares pride of place with an antique stool in the main living area of her home.

This is where she can indulge her fondness for preloved and recycled items. "Even if I don't need anything, I look forward to the possibilities," she says. "There is an endless supply of great pieces with charm and character, and the price is always right!" While furnishing her spaces, Sylvie relies on pieces with style, mellow finishes and time-honored materials rather than pedigree. These distinctive items make her home a collage of texture, sparkle and sentiment, as personal as it is peaceful. "When putting together a room, what matters is creating a comfortable, practical and aesthetically pleasing environment, which, for me, means layered, worn and authentic elements that make my home uniquely mine."

While the addition of the upstairs master suite, built by local masons, barely changed the original 1,200-square-foot/111-square-meter footprint, it did add a small tower to the single-story dwelling, enhancing the home's visual appeal.

The remaining challenge was to integrate the cottage into the surrounding Provençal landscape. "My aim was to create several distinct areas where I could relax, dine or entertain outdoors, surrounded by flowers and greenery," says Sylvie. At first, only the sweet scent of lavender and large pots of aromatic herbs surrounded her oases of calm. But she soon added quick-growing trees and shrubs, which in time contributed to the lush, romantic look.

Although the farmhouse she purchased was not the cottage she was looking for originally, it turned out to be the home Sylvie had always wanted. With its soothing palette and imaginative decor, it is a tribute to her understated elegance, ingenuity and heritage.

PAGES 142–143 French textiles, such as the toile de Jouy *boutis* (quilt) seen here on the bed, are unsurpassed in their craftsmanship and sense of place. The bed's turned posts likewise highlight local artisanal workmanship. The apothecary cabinet was formerly used to store medicines and the tools of the trade. Childhood photos of Sylvie and her sister keep their bond ever present.

OPPOSITE Past and present coexist in the newly built master suite on the mezzanine level. A vintage sideboard was refinished and fitted with a modern basin. Old homes are notorious for their lack of storage, so Sylvie included a double closet. A large free-standing bathtub was another must-have.

ABOVE The master bedroom has a cozy atmosphere with its sloping ceiling and planked floor. Though small, it has room for a desk and chair and two trunks doubling as side tables. The white French bed linens get a touch of color from the cross-stitched pillows, which Sylvie made herself.

ABOVE Extending an overhang and adding walls on either side has created an outdoor room that the French would call a *salon d'été*. Sylvie has outfitted this sheltered area with all the comforts of an indoor living space, including comfortable furnishings and accoutrements. These rest on limestone gravel, as is the custom in Provence.

RIGHT An old zinc fountain offers a soothing water element. The limestone patio is a cool surface for barefoot living. Traditional window shutters are also used to screen the front doorway. Vintage iron beds have been cut down to make one-of-a-kind garden chairs and footstools.

"My aim was to create several distinct areas where I could relax, dine or entertain outdoors, surrounded by flowers and greenery."

Emotional ATTACHMENT

THOUGH IT WAS RATHER DATED, THE APPEAL OF THIS 1912 COTTAGE IN THE GROUNDS OF A FORMER DAIRY FARM IN COASTAL CALIFORNIA DIDN'T ESCAPE DARRIELLE AYRES WHEN SHE FIRST SAW IT OVER 20 YEARS AGO. "IT WAS ONLY TWO MILES FROM THE PACIFIC—I COULD HEAR AND SMELL THE OCEAN, WHICH I LOVE. I WAS ALSO TAKEN BY THE NICELY PEAKED ROOF, ORIGINAL WINDOWS AND OLD SHINGLE SIDING," DARRIELLE REMINISCES. "AND IT WAS LARGE ENOUGH TO ACCOMMODATE CHILDREN AND PETS."

The house had not been occupied for many years and was in need of an overhaul, but Darrielle was just the right person for the job. She grew up on a 600-acre/243-hectare horse ranch and learned early on that hard work and a can-do attitude will get you far, and that has always been her work ethic. When she first saw the house, she recalls, "the idea of fixing it up was exciting." Fortunately, the cottage had been moved here from a different part of the property in the 1980s and the foundation, electrics and plumbing had all been updated at that time. "Structurally, everything was in good condition—only the roof needed to be replaced, which we did while keeping its original line."

Darrielle also made a few changes to the internal layout to open up the space. "When we bought the house, the front entrance was really the side entrance and there was an enclosed porch. This was reconfigured into a front porch and entry. A few walls were removed to enlarge the kitchen, the master bedroom was extended to allow for more space and French doors were added to the living room."

OPPOSITE Except for the sofa, everything in Darrielle's living room was found at flea markets. She refinished all the tables and used vintage fabrics to make the pillows and upholster the armchair. The green shutters have kept their original paint.

ABOVE Evocative coastal items, including seascapes, glass floats, shells and blue hues, are intrinsic elements of Darrielle's decor. "I have lived my entire life near the water, and those colors bring me comfort, pleasure and peace," she says.

BELOW & RIGHT Darrielle has a knack for vintage shopping and a keen eye for pieces with possibilities. But what makes her finds so special is her ability to rework and transform them to create cozy, layered and character-rich spaces. Here, she has brought together a shapely mirror from a flea market, a repainted mantel, a re-covered armchair and an old trunk that she found 20 years ago.

OPPOSITE French doors from the living and dining areas open to a light-filled family room where a vintage chandelier watches over a piano—a gift from Darrielle's father to her daughter. An elegant flea-market chair and a bench have been reupholstered using old linen grain sacks, which Darrielle bought in Paris. Oil paintings like the pair hanging on the wall are among her favorite items to collect.

The new doors open onto a large deck, which is not the only new addition to the formerly neglected outdoor space. "The previous owner was a developer who was going to build new houses on the land, so the yard was just construction dirt," recalls Darrielle. "With time and work, it has evolved and many plants and flowers were added." The old, dark brown shingles on the exterior walls have also been cleaned and spruced up with white paint.

"Many hours were spent on painting, sanding and numerous other do-it-yourself interior projects," says Darrielle. "It took a while to save up and complete the renovation. Over time, my vision for the cottage has changed, but what has stayed the same is that I still want my home to be comfortable, cozy and easy to live in. I like bright, cheerful spaces that make you feel at home. I feel like I have achieved that consistently throughout the years of living here."

RIGHT Above the vintage bench, a painting of Mendocino, Darrielle's hometown in California, was a gift. The farmhouse table was custom made to fit comfortably within the narrow room. Darrielle refinished the found sideboard with white chalk paint. The curvaceous, rusty chandelier is a European antique.

Growing up on an old ranch and with little money played a big role in Darrielle's appreciation for vintage and her affinity for refurbishing found or secondhand items. She seeks out flea markets, thrift stores and barn and yard sales, but also counts a few local stores among her favorite treasure hunting spots.

"I have always loved flowers and floral fabrics—even when I was a young child, I picked out the floral bedding and curtains for my canopy bed," she explains. "I've always felt that having beauty around me in my spaces, especially my home, is important. If I am going to have things in my personal space, then I want them to be visually pleasing and have beauty as well as a functional purpose."

Thanks to Darrielle's care and attention, the years have been kind to the little cottage. It's a charming and joyful home and with its watery hues embodies her love for the romance of coastal living.

LEFT The cozy built-in banquette is a charming addition to this small breakfast area. As for the preloved chairs, Darrielle says, "they get repainted periodically depending on the mood of the moment." The stormy seascape and blue-hued textiles reflect her love of coastal colors.

OPPOSITE The light-filled bedroom is one of Darrielle's favorite spaces. She is particularly proud of the headboard, which she built herself using 100-year-old planks that were discovered during the remodeling phase. The bench imparts a little luxury in contrast to the more rustic furnishings.

PAGE 156 On the other side of the bedroom, Darrielle worked her magic again, this time building the sliding barn door herself. She painted the wood using different colors with a salt wash to create a weathered finish. She also gave the vintage credenza/sideboard a coat of milk paint and added a marble top and basin. The flea-market mirror completes the look.

PAGE 157 After giving he salvaged clawfoot tub a thorough cleaning, Darrielle opted to keep its rusty exterior finish for a sense of authenticity. Painted stools add to the bathroom's cottage appeal, while artworks and accessories in bright aqua shades recall the waves of the nearby Pacific Ocean.

"I like bright, cheerful spaces that make you feel at home."

Index

Page numbers in *italics* refer
to illustrations

Picture credits

All photography by Mark Lohman unless otherwise stated.

Key: Ph = photographer; **a** = above; **b** = below; **l** = left; **c** = center; **r** = right.

Endpapers The home of Isabella and Robert Nelson in Sarasota, Florida; **1 & 2** The home of Darrielle Ayres in California; **3** The home of Deborah Yonemura in California; **4** The home of Isabella and Robert Nelson in Sarasota, Florida; **5** The home of Fifi O'Neill in Florida; **6 l** The home of Doré Callaway in California; **6 c** The home of Darrielle Ayres in California; **6 r** The home of Fifi O'Neill in Florida; **7** The home of Darrielle Ayres in California; **8–9** The home of Deborah Yonemura in California; **10** The home of Darrielle Ayres in California; **11 al** The loft of Teresa DeJarlais in Minnesota; **11 ac** The home of Janet and Larry Solomon in San Clemente, California; **11 ar** The home of Deborah Yonemura in California; **11 bl** The home of Valerie Madeira in California; **11 bc** The home of Fifi O'Neill in Florida; **11 br** The home of Janet and Larry Solomon in San Clemente, California; **12 a & bl** The home of Isabella and Robert Nelson in Sarasota, Florida; **12 br & 13** The home of Fifi O'Neill in Florida; **14** The home of Doré Callaway in California; **15 l** Ph John Ellis/The home of Sylvie Sommer in France; **15 r** The home of Deborah Yonemura in California; **16 a** The home of Darrielle Ayres in California; **16 b** The home of Janet and Larry Solomon in San Clemente, California; **17** The home of Marie Samuels in Rhode Island; **18 ar** The home of Isabella and Robert Nelson in Sarasota, Florida; **18 bl** The home of Fifi O'Neill in Florida; **18 br** The home of Janet and Larry Solomon in San Clemente, California; **19 & 20** The home of Doré Callaway in California; **21 l & r** The home of Fifi O'Neill in Florida; **22** The home of Janet and Larry Solomon in San Clemente, California; **23 al** The home of Valerie Madeira in California; **23 bl** The home of Deborah Yonemura in California; **23 r** The home of Isabella and Robert Nelson in Sarasota, Florida; **24 al** Ph John Ellis/The home of Sylvie Sommer in France; **24 ar** The home of Isabella and Robert Nelson in Sarasota, Florida; **24 b** The home of Doré Callaway in California; **25** The home of Valerie Madeira in California; **26 al, ac & ar** The home of Fifi O'Neill in Florida; **26 bl** The home of Valerie Madeira in California; **26 br** The home of Janet and Larry Solomon in San Clemente, California; **27** The home of Isabella and Robert Nelson in Sarasota, Florida; **28 a** The home of Janet and Larry Solomon in San Clemente, California; **28 b & 29** The home of Isabella and Robert Nelson in Sarasota, Florida; **30–31** The home of Isabella and Robert Nelson in Sarasota, Florida; **32–43** The loft of Teresa DeJarlais in Minnesota; **44–55** The home of Deborah Yonemura in California; **56–63** The home of Doré Callaway in California; **64–77** The home of Marie Samuels in Rhode Island; **78–87** The home of Kelley Motschenbacher in California; **88–99** The home of Isabella and Robert Nelson in Sarasota, Florida; **100–109** The home of Janet and Larry Solomon in San Clemente, California; **110–121** The home of Fifi O'Neill in Florida; **122–135** The home of Valerie Madeira in California; **136–147** Ph John Ellis/The home of Sylvie Sommer in France; **148–157 & 160** The home of Darrielle Ayres in California.

Business credits

DARRIELLE AYRES
Clementine & Co.
126 San Jose Ave
Capitola, CA 95010
Instagram: @ddscottage

ISABELLA AND ROBERT NELSON
Bon Bon Vintage
www.ilovebonbon.com
Instagram: @bonbonvintagesarasota
Facebook: @bonbonvintage

DORÉ CALLAWAY
INTERIOR DESIGN
www.etsy.com/shop/burlapluxe
dh4design@aol.com
Instagram: @BurlapLuxe

TERESA DEJARLAIS
The Porch in Buffalo
www.theporchinbuffalo.com
Instagram: @theporchinbuffalo
Facebook: @theporchinbuffalo

VALERIE MADEIRA
Valerie's Vintage & Supply Co.
www.valeriesvintageandsupply.com
Instagram: @valeriesvintage17

KELLEY MOTSCHENBACHER
Blu Canoe
www.theblucanoe.com
www.blucanoestudio.com
Instagram: @the_blu_canoe
Facebook: @theblucanoe

MARIE SAMUELS
Instagram: @Mariesamuels18

JANET SOLOMON
My Bleu Door
www.etsy.com/shop/MyBleuDoor

DEBORAH YONEMURA
Instagram: @thejoyofbeautifulliving

Acknowledgments

A book on interiors can only happen when homeowners agree to have their homes photographed. It's not as simple as it seems because many factors come into the process—schedules, travels, weather and a myriad of other unpredictable events. However, these generous people always figure a way to make it possible. Once again, my photographer Mark Lohman rose to the challenge, and we flew from coast to coast where we were welcomed with open arms (and food and drinks)!

Though I have been in hundreds of homes over the years, I am still moved by the warm and caring attention each of the homeowners bestowed on us. So, to begin with, my heartfelt thanks to Deborah and David Yonemura, Doré Callaway, Teresa DeJarlais, Isabella and Robert Nelson, Valerie and Mike Madeira,

Kelley and Greg Motschenbacher, Marie and William Samuels, Janet and Larry Solomon, Sylvie Sommer and Darrielle Ayres.

Then comes the work of laying out the lovely photographs, which is where art director Sally Powell and designer Toni Kay make magic happen. Thank you, ladies, for the beauty you create. Let's not forget Sophie Devlin, my wonderful editor who always makes me a better writer. Sophie, working with you is always a pleasure. Last but definitely not least, a most special thank you to senior commissioning editor Annabel Morgan, creative director Leslie Harrington and production manager Gordana Simakovic.

With love and gratitude to all.
Fifi